Copyright

To my momma who sparked the fire in me to do what I do, I love you momma.

The Beginning

I remember always in the kitchen watching my momma doing her thing, from making greens, pig's feet, fried chicken, catfish and many other Soul food items. She would always tell me "boy" you better be watching me so that you will know how to take care of yourself, no one knows how long I'm gonna be around and I want you to be able to take care of yourself and not count on anyone. As I rolled my eyes and said yes ma'am , I must say that I have been blessed to still have my momma with me, and I continue to use all her teaching when it comes to love, life and of course Soul Food.

Soul food is more than just a name or a cooking style it's a way of life, having the whole family coming together for communion and fellowship. Using recipes handed down from my great grandmother Momma Agnes and her mother Momma Jones. With all these skills passed down to me I had no other choice but to succeed in the culinary business.

BASIC RULES OF KITCHEN SAFETY

Cooking is fun, but kitchen safety is a priority. There are many pieces of equipment and environmental hazards that can be extremely dangerous. Sharp objects like knives, open fire by the oven, electrical appliances, and even bacteria around the kitchen. Observing basic rules of **kitchen safety** is a good habit to develop. Always pay attention to what you're doing in the kitchen because one slip can cause serious injury or accidents. To prevent serious injuries or accidents: always pay attention to what you're doing, adopt a plan for kitchen cleanliness, and have necessary safety equipment at your disposal. It's also important to be aware of who is in the space – for example, children should never be left alone in the kitchen!

- **Store knives in a wooden block or in a drawer.** Make sure the knives are out of the reach of children. Follow these knife safety tips to prevent injury.

- **Never cook in loose clothes and keep long hair tied back.** You don't want anything accidentally catching fire (not to mention hair ending up in the food!).
- **Never cook while wearing dangling jewelry.** A bracelet can get tangled around pot handles.
- **Keep potholders nearby and use them!** Be careful not to leave them near an open flame.
- **Turn pot handles away from the front of the stove.** Children can't grab them, and adults can't bump into them if they're out of the way.
- **Don't let temperature-sensitive foods sit out in the kitchen.** Raw meat, fish, and certain dairy products can spoil quickly, so refrigerate or freeze them right away.
- **Wipe up spills immediately.** Keep the floor dry so that no one slips and falls.

- **Separate raw meat and poultry from other items whenever you use or store them.** This precaution avoids cross-contamination of harmful bacteria from one food to another.
- **Wash your hands before handling food and after handling meat or poultry.** Hands can be a virtual freight train of bacteria.
- **Get a fire extinguisher for your kitchen.** This device may not do much for your cherries jubilee, but it can avert a disaster. You should do your best to prevent a kitchen fire, but sometimes it's out of your hands. So, make sure you know how to use the extinguisher before a fire breaks out. You can't waste any time reading the directions amidst the flames.

Kitchen essentials

Spoons, Ladles, and More

- **Ladle**
  Look for a large "bowl" that makes it easy to serve soups. Also, a bent handle at the top allows you to hook the ladle on the side of a pot without it falling in.
- **Locking tongs**
  Select a style with nonslip handles and scalloped tips for a firm grip. Use for turning meats and tossing vegetables in a skillet.
- **Metal spatula**
  An offset thin blade will allow you to get under delicate items like cookies and pancakes. A medium-length blade will prevent flipping or picking up foods at an awkward angle.
- **Rubber spatula**
  Should be sturdy enough to maneuver heavy doughs but flexible enough to get into jar corners. Silicone models are heat-resistant and can be used in pots.
- **Slotted spoon**
  Pick a sturdy spoon with a stainless steel handle that won't get too hot.

- **Whisk**
  A solid rather than a wired handle will prevent food from getting stuck inside. Buy one with thin wires (not thick, heavy ones) to make sure it's well-balanced when whipping egg whites or cream.

For Slicing

- **Chef's knife**
  Opt for an 8- to 9-inch blade with a thick bolster, the metal that extends from the handle to the edge of the blade and acts as a finger guard while you're chopping. This knife should feel comfortable in your hand.
- **Garlic press**
  A nice shortcut while chopping: one that works on unpeeled cloves and is dishwasher-safe.
- **Grater**
  A box grater is the most versatile with six different grate options to shred, shave, dust, and zest. Choose one with a sturdy handle.
- **Kitchen shears**
  Invest in a sturdy pair with tapered, fine tips and roomy handles.
- **Lemon press**
  The best models are big enough for both a lime and a lemon and have ridges to grip fruit better.
- **Microplane grater**
  For small tasks that require a fine grater—zesting lemons and grating Parmesan, garlic, and nutmeg—use a razor-sharp, stainless steel model.
- **Paring knife**
  The blade should fall between 3 to 4 inches for small, fine cuts like coring tomatoes and peeling fruits and vegetables. A sturdy model's blade will extend through the handle.
- **Potato masher**

A curved head will let you get into corners of bowls and pots.

- **Serrated bread knife**
  You want a rigid blade of at least 8 inches and an offset handle, which will let you slice through sandwiches without banging your knuckles on the cutting board.
- **Y-shaped vegetable peeler**
  This will give you a better grip than a traditional swivel model for hard-to-peel foods like mangoes and butternut squash.

Other Equipment

- **Can opener**
  A safe-cut, or smooth-edge, model cuts around the outside of the can, rather than the lid; produces smooth edges; and will never lower the lid into your food.
- **Corkscrew**
  A standard waiter's corkscrew will open both beer and wine and take up much less space than a two-armed model.
- **Instant-read thermometer**
  Find one that is easy-to-read and shatterproof.
- **Measuring cups**
  You'll want measuring cups for both dry and wet ingredients. For dry ingredients, you'll need at least 1-cup and 4-cup measuring tools on hand.
- **Measuring spoons**
  Oval models are more likely to fit into spice jars.
- **Peppermill**
  An easily adjustable grind setting will let you go from coarse to fine. A large hole allows easy refilling of the peppercorns.
- **Salad spinner**

You can use one with a solid bowl for both swishing greens clean and serving them.

- **Timer**
  Some digital models allow for multiple timekeepings, so you can track a roast in the oven, potatoes on the stovetop, and dough in the refrigerator—all at the same time.
- **Wire mesh colanders**
  Buy one with a foot at the bottom to ensure your pasta won't sit in the residual puddle in the sink. You can use a small one as a flour sifter in a pinch.

Soul Food

When I was a little kid there was nothing like running into the house to my mom's cooking and smelling the Southern Creations that filled the air. Her fried chicken, pork chops, meatloaf, and pig's feet were the main dishes that are the staple of Soul Food in our family.

Entrées

Mommas Buttermilk Brined Southern Fried Chicken

Serves 4-6

Ingredients
8 pieces of chicken (I cut up whole chickens from Hoe Hop Valley farm, and used the breasts, legs, and thighs. I also cut the breasts in half horizontally because they were large)

Brine
1 quart buttermilk (I will have a recipe to follow)

1 cup water
1/8 cup kosher salt
1 Tbsp Chef Stacks Creole Seasoning7
1 Tbsp Frank's Hot Sauce
1/4 tsp freshly grated nutmeg
1/4 cup honey
¼ Tsp Paprika to taste (optional)
A few sprigs of thyme
Coating
3 cups flour
3 tsp baking powder
3 Tbsp cornstarch
1-2 tsp Sea salt
1/2 tsp freshly grated black pepper
1/4 tsp dry mustard
1/4 tsp cayenne
1/4 tsp paprika
2 tsp garlic powder

2 cups buttermilk
Oil for frying (you need enough to come about 1/3 of the way up the pot or 2 inches)
{Note: I have used both vegetable and canola oil successfully}
Kosher salt for sprinkling
Directions
For the brine: Combine all the ingredients for the brine except buttermilk in a small pot and heat over medium, dissolving all the salt and honey. Remove from heat and cool by adding ice cubes and stirring. In a large mixing bowl combine buttermilk and cooled seasoned water. Rinse chicken and pat dry. Divide all pieces of chicken between two large zip lock bags. Pour half of buttermilk brine in each, close, and place in the refrigerator overnight, up to 12 hours. I have left them in there longer, 14-15 hours, with no ill effects. {note: I have also halved the brine recipe and used one large zip lock for 8 pieces of chicken and it worked out well, a good way to save.}
1-2 hours before you are ready to fry: Rinse the chicken under cold water and pat dry. Let the chicken come to room temperature, half an hour to one and a half hours, on a parchment lined baking sheet covered with paper towels. Preheat oven to 350°.
Mix all of the ingredients for the coating together in a large bowl, transferring half to a second bowl. {note: The measurements given for seasonings here are approximate. I season my flour to taste. Yes, I taste the raw flour. It should taste salty & flavorful.} Fill a third bowl with the 2 cups of buttermilk. The easiest way to coat the chicken is to have a line set up: uncoated chicken, flour coating, buttermilk, 2nd bowl of flour coating, wax paper lined baking sheet for the coated chicken.
Pour the oil into your pot (preferably cast iron). It should come at least two inches and no more than 1/3 of the way up the side of the pot. Turn the heat to low, clipping a frying/candy thermometer to the side of your pot.
Dredge each piece in the coating, dust off all excess, dip into the buttermilk, and then into the second bowl of coating,

letting the 2nd coating be clumpier but still patting to get rid of excess that might fall off in the oil. Place coated chicken on the wax paper lined tray.

Turn the oil up to high and let it come to about 350° F. Let the coated chicken sit so that the coating will thicken while the oil gets hot. When it reaches temperature, very carefully place 4 pieces of chicken at a time in the hot oil and fry, adjusting the temperature as needed to maintain a frying temperature between 310° -325° F. I try to keep it around 320°. You start the oil at 350° because when you add the chicken to the hot oil, the temperature will drop. Fry dark meat first, as it takes longer. Fry the chicken for about 13-20 minutes, moving the chicken gently (you don't want to knock the coating off!) after the first five to prevent sticking and burning on the bottom. Be careful to monitor your chicken, watching the oil temperature closely and not letting the chicken get too dark.

Remove chicken from the oil with a spider or slotted metal spoon when it is golden brown (metal tongs will knock off your precious coating), and place it on a cooling rack over a paper towel lined baking sheet. Sprinkle with kosher salt. Check the internal temperature with an instant read thermometer. Fully cooked chicken will read 160 degrees and can be served then if desired. If it is lower than that, it must be finished in the oven. Fry the second batch and then place it on the rack. Place the rack in the oven for ten minutes. Check the internal temperature to make sure the chicken is cooked through, let rest 10 minutes, and serve hot. If all the chicken is cooked through and you want to keep it hot, you can hold it in a 250 degree oven

Buttermilk

Ingredients

- **2 tablespoons freshly squeezed lemon juice or white vinegar**
- **1 Cup (8oz / 224g) milk (full or low fat)**

How to make it

- **Measure the milk into a jug**
- **Stir in lemon juice or vinegar into the milk. Stir to combine. Let sit for 30 minutes at room temperature until the milk begins to curdle and becomes acidic**

Creole sauce

- 2 tablespoons olive oil
- 1 cup diced onions (about 1 medium)
- 1/2 cup diced celery (about 2 stalks)
- 1/2 cup diced green bell pepper (about 1 medium)
- 1 tablespoon minced garlic (about 3 medium cloves)
- 1 (14 ounce) can diced tomatoes
- 2 cups low-sodium store-bought or homemade chicken stock
- 1 tablespoon Louisiana-style hot sauce (such as Frank's or Crystal), plus more to taste
- 1 tablespoon Worcestershire sauce
- 2 bay leaves
- 1/4 teaspoon ground white pepper
- 1/4 teaspoon cayenne pepper
- 1/2 teaspoon dried thyme leaves
- 4 tablespoons butter
- 2 tablespoons finely chopped fresh parsley leaves
- 1/2 cup thinly sliced green onions
- Kosher salt and freshly ground black pepper

How to do it

-

Heat oil in large saucepan over medium-high heat until shimmering. Add onions, celery, and green peppers and cook, stirring occasionally, until vegetables start to soften, 3 to 5 minutes. Stir in garlic and cook until fragrant, about 30 seconds.

- Stir in tomatoes, stock, hot sauce, Worcestershire sauce, bay leaves, white pepper, cayenne pepper, and thyme. Bring to a boil, then reduce heat to low. Simmer until sauce slightly thickens, about 20 minutes.

- With salt, pepper, and additional hot sauce to taste. Sauce will keep in a seal bay leaves. Add butter and stir until completely melted. Remove from heat. Remove and discard and stir in parsley and green onions. Seasoned container in the refrigerator for up to 1 week.

Cajun Crab Cakes

Ingredients

- *For the Crab Cakes:*
- 2 tablespoons salted butter
- 1/2 onion, finely chopped
- 2 stalks celery, finely chopped
- 1/2 large red bell pepper, finely chopped
- 1 bunch green onions (green portion only), chopped
- 1/2 large carrot, finely chopped
- 3 cloves garlic, minced
- 1 tablespoon parsley flakes
- 2 teaspoons Creole seasoning (Chef Stacks Recipe)
- 2 teaspoons dried basil
- 2 teaspoons ground black pepper
- 1 teaspoon dried dill weed
- 1/2 teaspoon oregano
- 1/2 teaspoon dried thyme
- 2 large eggs, beaten
- 1 pound lump crabmeat, picked free of shell
- 9 buttery crackers (such as Keebler Club® crackers), crushed
- 3 tablespoons vegetable oil
- *For the Spicy Cajun Dipping Sauce:*
- 1 cup mayonnaise
- 1 tablespoon chile-garlic sauce (such as Sriracha®)
- 2 teaspoons Creole seasoning (Chef Stacks Recipient)
- 2 teaspoons parsley flakes
- 1 teaspoon paprika
- Add all ingredients to list

How to make it

- Prep
  40 m

- Cook
  20 m
- Ready In
  1 h 30 m
- Melt butter in a large, heavy skillet over medium heat. Stir in onion; cook and stir until the onion has softened and turned translucent, about 5 minutes.
- Stir in the celery, bell pepper, green onion, carrot, and garlic. Continue to cook and stir until vegetables are tender, about 10 minutes more.
- Season with 1 tablespoon parsley flakes, 2 teaspoons Creole seasoning, basil, pepper, dill weed, oregano, and thyme. Cook and stir until fragrant, 5 minutes more.
- Transfer cooked vegetables to a large bowl; allow to cool for about 10 minutes. Set skillet aside for later use.
- Stir the beaten eggs into the vegetables. Mix in the crabmeat and cracker crumbs with your hands, making sure not to break up the chunks of crab too much.
- Shape the crab mixture into 12 small cakes.
- Heat vegetable oil in the skillet over medium high heat.
- Pan-fry the crab cakes in batches until golden brown on each side, about 3 minutes.
- To make dipping sauce: Whisk together the mayonnaise, chili-garlic sauce, 2 teaspoon Creole seasoning, 2 teaspoon parsley flakes, and paprika

Maple Bourbon Chicken an Waffle Sandwich

INGREDIENTS

For waffles

- **3 large eggs, whites and yolks separated**
- **2 boxes cornbread mix**
- **½ c. all-purpose flour**
- **½ c. baking soda**
- **1 c. milk**
- **2 tbsp. honey**
- **4 tbsp. butter, melted**

For Fried Chicken

- **1 lb. chicken cutlets, sliced in half**
- **1 c. buttermilk**
- **1 tbsp. Hot sauce**
- **1½ c. all-purpose flour**
- **2 tsp. garlic powder**
- **1 tsp. paprika**
- **kosher salt or sea salt**
- **Freshly ground black pepper**
- **Vegetable oil, for frying**

FOR THE MAPLE BOURBON SYRUP

- 2 oz. bourbon whisky
- 8 oz. pure maple syrup
- 3 tbsp. butter

DIRECTIONS

- Make the waffles: Preheat the waffle iron . Whisk egg whites to soft peaks and set aside. Whisk all other waffle ingredients together and fold in egg whites. Depending on the size of your waffle iron, use a 1/3 to 1/2 cup measure to pour batter onto hot iron. Cook until crispy and browned.

- Fry the chicken: In a bowl, marinate chicken in buttermilk with a few dashes of hot sauce. In a separate bowl, mix flour with garlic powder and paprika, and season with salt and pepper. Dredge chicken in the flour. In a cast-iron pan over medium-high heat, add 1 inch of oil and fry chicken cutlets. Once golden brown and cooked through, remove to a paper towel to drain.

- Make the syrup: In a small saucepan, add bourbon and maple syrup. Heat on medium-high heat to burn off alcohol and reduce liquid (about 5 minutes). Remove from heat and whisk in butter. Let cool to room temperature or slightly warm before serving.

- **Assemble the sandwiches: Place a piece of fried chicken in between two waffles and top with bourbon sauce. Serve with bacon**

The Greg Page Roast Beef Po Boi with TKO Gravy

The Bread

Use two large French Bread loaves, either homemade, or locally purchased. Around Louisville , we often use a New Orleans style po'boy bread, though a good deli French bread from the grocery store like Kroger or super center works just fine too. Substitute any long Italian or French bread loaf that is not too dense - you want it light and airy inside.

Ingredients

The Roast:

- 1 (2-3 pound) beef eye of round roast
- Water to cover, do not discard

For the Gravy:

- 4 cups of the reserved broth from the roast, plus extra as needed
- 1/2 cup of all-purpose flour
- 1/2 teaspoon of Chef Stacks Cajun seasoning recipe
- 1/2 teaspoon of onion salt
- 1/2 tablespoon of garlic powder
- 1 teaspoon of kosher salt
- 1/4 teaspoon of freshly cracked black pepper, or to taste

- 1/4 cup of canola oil
- Couple sprigs of fresh thyme

Building the Po'Boy:

- French Bread
- Mississippi come back mayo (MCB mayo)
- Sliced Tomato
- Salt and pepper, to taste
- Sliced dill pickles, optional
- Shredded Iceberg lettuce

Instructions

For the roast, place meat in a pot or dutch oven and cover it with water, plus about an inch. Remove the roast and set aside. Bring the water up to a full rolling boil on it's own, and then, carefully slide the roast into it. When the water returns to a boil, reduce to a slow simmer and let cook for about 1-1/2 hours. Remove the roast, reserving all of the water from the broth; set aside. Place roast into the refrigerator to chill for easier slicing.

For the gravy, transfer 4 cups of the stock from the roast into a large saucepan. Bring to a boil. Meanwhile stir together the flour, Cajun seasoning, onion salt, garlic powder, salt and pepper until well blended. Stir in the oil and Kitchen Bouquet to form a thick paste.

Once the water is at a full rolling boil, quickly whisk in the paste and continue whisking until well incorporated. Reduce heat, add thyme, and low simmer the gravy uncovered, for 30 minutes, adding more of the broth water to reach the desired consistency. Taste and adjust seasonings as needed.

Preheat the oven to 325 degrees F. While the gravy is simmering, remove the roast from the refrigerator and slice it into very thin slices. Set aside approximately 1 cup of the gravy. Place one layer of roast beef into a 9 x 9 inch baking dish and top with a scoop of the gravy. Add another layer of roast beef, another scoop of the gravy, and continue layering until all has been put into the pan. Be sure to pan all of the bits and imperfect pieces from cutting (the debris). Cover the dish with aluminum foil and bake at 325 degrees F for about 1 hour, turning occasionally, or until meat is tender.

To build the po'boy, divide the French bread into halves or the size needed, and slice each piece lengthwise. Try to leave a flat edge "hinge" intact if possible. It sort of helps to hold everything in. If you cut through or it opens up anyway, no big deal! Heat a large cast iron or skillet, open the bread up and toast each serving on the inside.

Add the MCB mayo to both sides of the inside of the French bread for each serving. Add roast beef to the bottom half of the bread. Top with sliced tomatoes; add salt and pepper. Add pickles, if desired. Top with shredded lettuce, and place other half of the French bread on top. Place back into the skillet, and using a wide spatula, press down while heating. You can also use a press, if you can control the pressure, or you can put a heavy skillet on top. I prefer to just press with a wide spatula so not to squeeze out too much of the gravy! Carefully turn the po'boy over and repeat on the other side, toasting while pressing.

Transfer the po'boy to a cutting board and slice in half. Open and add some of the reserved gravy if desired. Wrap tightly in several sheets of white butcher paper, and serve with a side of Gripos potato chips, an ice cold, bottle of Big Red and a lot of napkins!
Now *that's* genuine!

CHEF STACK'S Notes: Shortcut the process by using deli sliced roast beef. Use 4 cups of beef broth to prepare gravy and proceed with the recipe.

Chef Stacks Cajun

Ingredients

- 2tablespoons onion powder
- 2tablespoons garlic powder
- 2tablespoons dried oregano
- 2tablespoons dried basil
- 1tablespoon dried thyme
- 1tablespoon fresh ground black pepper
- 1tablespoon white pepper (or 2 use tablespoons black pepper)
- 3teaspoons cayenne pepper
- 5tablespoons paprika
- 4 -5tablespoons seasoning salt (I use Lawry's seasoned salt for this

Chef Stacks Jambalaya

Ingredients

- 3 slices of bacon
- 1 pound of raw pork loin, cut into cubes
- 1 pound of andouille or other spicy smoked sausage, diced or sliced into 1/4 inch rounds
- 1/4 cup of water
- 2 cups of chopped onion
- 1 cup of chopped green bell pepper
- 1/4 cup of chopped celery
- 1 tablespoon of minced garlic
- 1 quart of beef stock or broth
- 3 cups of water, heated
- 1/4 cup of sliced green onion
- 1/4 teaspoon of Cajun seasoning (Chef Stacks Recipe), or to taste, *optional*
- 1/2 teaspoon of dried thyme
- 1/2 teaspoon of dried basil
- 1/2 tablespoon of dried parsley, plus extra for garnish if desired
- 4 cups of long grain rice
- Bottled hot pepper sauce, for the table

Instructions

Slice bacon into a 6 quart Dutch oven and cook until fat is rendered. Add the cubed pork and cook over medium high heat in the drippings, stirring regularly, until meat is heavily browned and browned bits (the fond) have formed in the bottom of the pot. Add the sausage, cook and stir for 3 minutes, add the 1/4 cup of water a little at a time, using a wooden spoon to scrape up the browned

bits from the bottom. This will add both flavor and color to your jambalaya.

Add the onion, bell pepper and celery, cook and stir for 4 minutes; add the garlic and cook another minute. Stir in the beef stock, bring mixture to a boil, reduce heat, cover and let simmer for 20 minutes. Meanwhile, preheat oven to 350 degrees F. Add the 3 cups of hot water, green onion, Cajun seasoning, thyme, basil, parsley and rice; stir well.

Cover and transfer pot to the oven, baking at 350 degrees F for 35 minutes. Remove and let stand covered until ready to serve, or for at least 10 minutes. Fluff with a fork before serving. Spoon loosely into a serving platter if desired, but do not pack down. Garnish with parsley, serve with a side salad or green vegetable, and pass a bottle of hot pepper sauce at the table.

CHEF STACK's Notes: With andouille sausage, and no additional cayenne pepper or Cajun seasoning, this results in what I would call a moderately spicy jambalaya with a healthy kick. Add cayenne pepper or Cajun/Creole seasoning for extra spicy. For testing purposes, I used Conecuh brand Cajun Smoked Sausage. For a milder dish, substitute a mild smoked sausage or kielbasa. Okay to substitute leftover cooked pork, or a loose raw sausage. Chopped baked ham may also be used.

Alice Pages

Chicken Pot pie

Ingredients

- 1 pound of cooked boneless, skinless chicken breasts or mixed chicken (about 2-1/2 cups cubed)
- 3 medium red potatoes, unpeeled
- 1/2 cup of frozen carrots
- 1/2 cup of frozen peas
- 6 tablespoons of salted butter
- 6 tablespoons of all-purpose flour
- 2 cups of chicken broth or stock
- 1/2 teaspoon of kosher salt
- About 8 turns of the pepper grinder
- 1/2 teaspoon of dried rosemary, crushed
- 1/2 teaspoon of dried thyme, crushed
- 1-1/2 cups of half and half
- 2 box of your favorite refrigerated pie crusts, softened to room temperature

Instructions

Preheat oven to 425 degrees F. Chop the potatoes into small cubes and place into a microwave safe dish. Cook on high for about 2-1/2 minutes or until tender. Set aside. In another microwave safe dish, add the carrots and peas; microwave on high for about 2 minutes, or until tender. Add to the potatoes.

In a large skillet, heat the butter over medium heat; add the flour in a tablespoon at a time, stirring in before adding the next. Cook, stirring constantly until mixture is bubbly and there are no remaining lumps, about 5 minutes. Slowly begin to incorporate the chicken stock, stirring vigorously until fully incorporated. Add in the seasonings and stir in well. Remove from heat, add the salt, pepper, rosemary and thyme. Stir in the half and half until smooth.

Stir the chicken into the cream mixture, then add the potatoes, the carrots and peas; mix well. Taste and adjust seasonings as needed. Unroll one of the pie crusts and place into a 9-inch, ungreased deep dish, glass pie plate. Gently press the crust down into the bottom and edges of the pie plate. Pour the hot filling into the crust and top with the remaining crust, tucking the top crust up under the edges of the bottom crust. Flute the edges and cut vents into the top of the crust.

Bake immediately at 425 degrees F for 15 minutes. Remove and place strips of foil around the edges of the crust to prevent overbrowning. Return to oven for an additional 15 to 25 minutes, or until crust is golden brown and filling is bubbling. Let stand for 5 minutes before cutting.

CHEF STACKS's Notes: Use a deep dish pie plate for this recipe. Make sure that the oven is preheated and at temperature before filling the pie crust, because you want to fill the pie, top it and put it into the oven immediately to bake. May also make into individual pot pies.

Bobby Logan's Fried Catfish

This dish is from my best friend who is the catfish man of Kentucky.

Ingredients:

- **6-8 catfish fillets**
- **1 teaspoon garlic powder**
- **1 teaspoon black pepper**
- **2 teaspoons seasoned salt**
- **3/4 teaspoon onion powder**
- **1/2 teaspoon paprika**
- **2 cups cracker meal or crushed saltine crackers**
- **1 cup vegetable oil**

Cookware and Utensils:

- **1 cast iron skillet or large heavy skillet**
- **1 cutting board**
- **1 rolling pin**

Recipe Instructions:

As always the key to great cooking is to be prepared and to use quality ingredients.

- **Rinse fillets under running cold and then thoroughly pat dry with paper towels.**
- **Make your seasoning mixture by combining garlic powder, black pepper, seasoned salt, onion powder and paprika in a small bowl.**
- **Sprinkle seasoning mixture over both sides of the fillets. Next apply cracker meal by gently pressing the meal on both sides of your fillets.**

  Place fillets on a plate and refrigerate for about 1 hour to allow meal to coat properly.
- **Heat vegetable oil in a cast iron skillet or large heavy skillet. Fry the fillets on both sides until they are golden brown, turning only once. Allow fillets**

Sunday
Dinner's Baked Ham

Coming home from church and you smell that honey baked ham..... Now that's soul food

Ingredients:

- **1 - 8 to 10 pound smoked ham**
- **whole cloves**

Glaze for Baked Ham

- **1/2 cup honey**
- **1/2 cup orange juice**
- **1 cup packed light brown sugar**

Recipe Instructions:

- **Preheat oven according to package cooking directions. Place ham fat side up on the rack of a shallow roasting pan. Insert meat thermometer through fat side into center of thickest part of the ham, but don't let it touch the bone.**

- **Bake ham according to package directions. About 1/2 hour before ham is done prepare glaze by combining ingredients and mixing well. Next remove ham from oven and pour off drippings. Peel away any rind that is left on ham and score ham with a sharp knife.**
- **While scoring make diamond shaped cuts. Insert a clove into each diamond. Spread ham generously with glaze and return to oven. After applying glaze, bake until desired internal temperature is reached.**
- **Remove ham from oven and allow to stand for about 20 minutes before slicing. If desired, remaining glaze can be poured over sliced ham.**

Makes 10 to 12 servings.

My old man's favorite "Liver and Onions"

This was one of daddy's favorite meals, he loved his liver and onions made with love drenched in mommas special gravy.

Recipe Ingredients:

- **1 pound sliced liver, half inch thick**
- **2 large onions**
- **1 teaspoon chopped marjoram**
- **1 teaspoon thyme**
- **1 teaspoon parsley flakes**
- **1 teaspoon seasoned salt**
- **1/2 teaspoon prepared mustard**
- **1/2 teaspoon ground black pepper**
- **1/2 cup flour**
- **1/2 cup vegetable oil**
- **ice cold milk**

Cookware and Utensils:

- **1 large heavy or cast iron skillet**
- **1 small mixing bowl**
- **1 medium food storage container**
- **1 measuring spoons**

Recipe Instructions:

As always the key to great cooking is to be prepared and to use quality ingredients.

- **Prepare your liver 1-hour before cooking.**
- **Rinse sliced liver under cold running water and place in ice-cold milk for about 40 minutes.**
- **Peel and slice onions, then set aside.**
- **In small mixing bowl combine together chopped marjoram, thyme, parsley flakes, seasoned salt, prepared mustard and black pepper. Crush and mix all of the ingredients together to form your seasoning mixture.**
- **After about 40 minutes, remove sliced liver from milk and pat dry with paper towels. Coat each piece of liver first with seasoning mixture and then with flour.**
- **Heat vegetable oil in a large heavy skillet over medium-high heat. Fry the liver to your desired doneness.**
- **Removed cooked liver and place on a warmed plate until onions are done. Place onions into skillet, season with salt and pepper and brown, turning occasionally.**

Southern Red Beans and

Ingredients:

- 1 pound red kidney beans
- 1 cup finely chopped onions
- 2 finely chopped garlic cloves
- 1 smoked ham hock
- 3/4 to 1 pound smoked sausage, sliced into bite sized pieces
- 4 cups cooked long-grain white rice
- Salt and pepper to taste

Cookware and Utensils:

- 1 large heavy bottom pot
- small skillet

Recipe Instructions:

As always the key to great cooking is to be prepared and to use quality ingredients.

- Pour beans onto counter top and remove any debris like stones or twigs that may be present. Rinse beans then add them to pot or bowl and cover with at least two inches of water. Allow beans to soak in water overnight for 8 hours minimum.
- Drain beans that have been sitting overnight, rinse twice with water and set aside for cooking.

- In a small skillet over medium-high heat, stir and cook onions and garlic in olive oil for about 4 minutes until onions are soft.
- Add beans, onion, garlic and ham hock to large heavy bottom stock or soup pot. Cover with at least two inches of water and cook uncovered over simmering heat for about two hours until beans are tender. Stir occasionally and don't allow water to boil out. If you must add water, add about 1/4 cup of boiling water to the pot. Repeat adding water as much as necessary.
- Add sausage and continue to cook for 30 minutes. Remove the bay leaf, add salt and pepper to taste.

Serve beans and sausage hot over steamed or boiled rice.

Chef Stacks Notes – to make this a complete meal serve with southern cornbread

Beef Stew Recipe

Recipe Ingredients:

- 1-1/2 pound cubed beef stew meat
- 1 teaspoon seasoned salt
- 1/2 teaspoon onion powder
- 1/2 teaspoon pepper
- 3 celery stalks, sliced
- 2 potatoes - cubed
- 2 carrots - cubed
- 1 can whole tomatoes
- 1 medium onion – chopped
- 3 tablespoon vegetable oil
- 1/2 cup all-purpose flour
- water

Cookware and Utensils:

- 1 crock pot
- 1 large frying pan
- 1 measuring spoons
- 1 measuring cup
- 1 small mixing bowl

Recipe Instructions:

As always the key to great cooking is to be prepared and to use quality ingredients.

- Start the recipe of with a little prep work. Cube your potatoes and carrots, chop the onion and slice up your celery stalks.
- Next give your beef stew a good rinsing in cold water and pat the meat dry with paper towels and set aside.

- **In a small bowl form your <u>seasoning mixture</u> by combining and mixing together seasoned salt, onion powder and black pepper. Season you meat using the mixture. Next apply a light coat of flour to the beef stew.**
- **Add vegetable oil to large frying pans and Sauté beef until all sides have browned.**
- **Transfer the beef stew to the crock pot and add whole tomatoes, potatoes, carrots and onions. Add enough water to cover ingredients. Stir to evenly distribute <u>ingredients</u>.**
- **Cook on low heat for 10-12 hours or high heat for 5-6 hours. The beef stew is done when the meat and potatoes are tender.**

Never have these when my brother Dorsey is around because your pot will all of a sudden become empty.

BBQ Pigs Feet “aka Trotters

Ingredients:

- **4 pigs feet, split in half lengthwise**
- **2 medium onions, chopped**
- **2 stalks celery, chopped**
- **1 garlic clove, chopped**
- **1 bay leaf**
- **1 teaspoon salt**
- **1/4 cup cider vinegar**
- **1/4 teaspoon pepper**
- **water**
- **Chef Stacks barbecue sauce**

Cookware and Utensils:

- **1 Dutch oven or large boiling pot**
- **1 slotted spoon**
- **1 baking pan**
- **1 cutting board**

- 1 measuring spoons

Recipe Instructions:

As always the key to great cooking is to be prepared and to use quality ingredients.

- Okay, so where do you buy pigs feet? Often times you will have to ask the grocery store butcher for the pigs feet because they're usually frozen and sometime stored in the back of the store.
- Begin by giving the pigs feet a good washing. For presentation purposes remove any unsightly hair that you observe. Yes pigs grow hair on the toes and feet just like humans. A disposable razor will remove the hair.
- Place all the ingredients in a large boiling pot and cover with water. Bring water to a boil over medium-high heat and then reduce heat to a simmer. Cover pot with lid and allow pigs feet to cook for about 2-1/2 hours. While your meat is cooking stir constantly and skim away any foam that develops.
- Preheat your oven to 325 degrees during the last 5 minutes of cooking your meat.
- Using a slotted spoon remove the pigs feet from the cooking juice. Try to keep the meat intact. Place the meat on a baking pan, in single layers with skin facing up. Also use the slotted spoon to remove some of the onions and spices from the cooking juice.
- Add the onions and spice to the top of the pigs feet and then apply a thick layer of your favorite barbecue sauce. Finally, place the

pan in the oven and bake for about 40 minutes, until meat is tender.

Chef Stackz Southern BBQ sauce

Ingredients

- ¼cup molasses
- 1cup ketchup
- ½cup brown sugar
- 4teaspoons liquid smoke
- ½teaspoon onion salt
- ½cup apple cider vinegar
- ½teaspoon dry mustard
- ½teaspoon garlic powder

Southern Pork Chops

Recipe Ingredients:

- 6 pork chops, 1 inch thick
- 2 teaspoons seasoned salt
- 2 teaspoons garlic powder
- 1-1/2 tablespoons prepared mustard
- 1 teaspoon paprika
- 1/2 teaspoon black pepper
- 1/2 cup flour
- 1/2 cup vegetable oil

Cookware and Utensils:

- 1 large heavy or cast iron skillet
- 1 measuring spoons

Recipe Instructions:

As always the key to great cooking is to be prepared and to use quality ingredients.

- Prepare pork chops 1-hour before cooking.
- Rinse pork chops thoroughly under cold running water. Pat your pork chops dry with paper towels and set aside.
- In a small mixing bowl combine together seasoned salt, garlic powder, prepared mustard, paprika and black pepper. Mix all of the ingredients together to form your seasoning mixture.
- Rub about 3/4 teaspoon of seasoning on each pork chop. Next thoroughly coat each piece of

meat with flour and set aside. Now that seasoning is applied, refrigerate pork chops for about 1 hour before cooking.

- Heat vegetable oil in heavy skillet over medium heat. When the skillet is hot, add pork chops and brown on both sides for 10-12 minutes. Removed cooked pork chops from skillet and set on paper towels to drain grease

Neck Bones and Rice

Ingredients:
1 large onion, diced
4 cloves of garlic, minced
1/2 bell pepper, diced
32 0z vegetable broth
3 to 4 lbs. of pork neck bones
2 cups of white rice
salt to taste
1 tsp. black pepper
1 Tbs. paprika
1 tsp. cumin
1 tsp. garlic powder
1 tsp. onion powder
2 cups of water

How to make it

- **Cook the vegetables for 5 minutes on medium heat.**
- **Add the neck bones and cook for another 5 minutes.**
- **Add the rest of the ingredients, except rice and bring to a low simmer.**
- **Cook for 2 1/2 to 3 hours, adding water when needed.**

Rice Instructions:

- **In a separate pot bring 4 cups of water to a boil.**
- **Add rice.**
- **Add 1/2 teaspoon of salt.**
- **Bring back to boil, then lower heat**

Chef Stacks Notes – another added wow factor is to have gravy with your Neck bones.

To Make Gravy:

- **Place 2 Tablespoons Butter and 1 Tablespoon Bacon Grease in a large skillet, let melt.**
- **Add 3 Tablespoons of All-Purpose Flour, stir constantly.**
- **Continue to stir and let flour brown to desired color. The longer it cooks, the darker it will get.**
- **Add the 1 cup of reserved stock from the cooking pot. Stir constantly.**
- **Let mixture simmer until it slightly thickens.**
- **Pour gravy over rice and neck bones.**

Momma Agnes's Corn Pudding

INGREDIENTS

2 14-15 oz. cans whole kennel corn
2 14-15 oz. cans cream corn
6 beaten eggs
1/2 cup all-purpose flour
1 cup granulated sugar
3/4 stick cooled melted unsalted butter
pinch of salt
1/2 tsp. pure vanilla extract
Cooking spray to spray your baking dish (I use Pam)

READY, SET GO:

Pre-heat oven to 400
Add all ingredients to a large bowl and stir together (add the cooled melted butter last so it doesn't cook the eggs)
Spray baking dish with cooking spray
Pour corn pudding mixture into baking dish and bake uncovered for 1 hour or until golden brown on top and butter is bubbling just a little on top

Shrimp bacon and cheese grits

INGREDIENTS

- 2 1/4 c. low-sodium chicken broth
- 2 c. water
- kosher salt
- 1 c. quick cooking grits
- 3 tbsp. unsalted butter
- 1/2 c. grated Parmesan
- 6 oz. bacon, cut into 1/4" slices
- 1 onion, diced
- 1 garlic clove, grated
- 1 lb. shrimp, peeled and deveined
- Freshly ground black pepper
- 2 scallions, thinly sliced

How to make it

- In a small pot over medium-high heat, bring 2 cups broth and 2 cups water to a boil. Add 1/2 tsp salt and slowly pour in grits while stirring to keep smooth. Cook according to package instructions. Stir in 1 tbsp butter and Parmesan. Keep warm.

- **Meanwhile, in a large cast-iron skillet over medium heat, cook bacon until brown. Place bacon on a plate and set aside, reserving 2 tbsp bacon fat.**

- **Cook onions and garlic over medium heat until softened, 4 minutes. Pour in 1/4 cup broth, bring to a boil, and simmer until slightly thickened, 3 to 4 minutes. Add shrimp and season with salt and black pepper. Stir until shrimp are pink and cooked through, turn off heat, and add 2 tbsp butter and scallions.**

- **Serve shrimp over grits with a spoonful of sauce. Top with crumbled bacon and scallions , and grated cheddar cheese**

Southern Succotash

Ingredients

- 3 medium ears corn
- 1/2 pound fresh or frozen baby butter (lima) beans
- 3 slices bacon, cooked and chopped, reserve drippings
- 1/2 cup chopped andouille or smoked ham or turkey, *optional*
- 1 cup sliced fresh or frozen okra, *thawed*
- 1 cup chopped Vidalia or other sweet onion
- 1/2 cup chopped sweet bell pepper (green, red, yellow, orange or combination)
- 1/2 tablespoon minced garlic
- 1/2 tablespoon brown sugar
- 1 teaspoon kosher salt, *or to taste*
- 1/4 teaspoon freshly cracked black pepper, *or to taste*
- 1/4 teaspoon Creole or Cajun seasoning, *or to taste, optional*
- 1 cup halved grape tomatoes
- 2 teaspoons fresh, chopped parsley
- 1 tablespoon unsalted butter, or 1/8 cup heavy cream

Instructions

Cook corn using your favorite method, or place whole, unhusked corn in microwave and cook on high for 12 minutes (1000 watt); use oven mitt to remove and set aside to cool. Meanwhile, add butter beans to a small saucepan and cover with water. Bring to a boil, boil for 3 minutes, reduce to simmer and cook for 15 minutes, or until mostly tender. Drain, setting aside 1/2 cup of the cooking water. Rinse beans and set aside. Use a sharp serrated knife to carefully cut off the root end of the corn, remove husks and silks and cut corn off of the cob. Use dull edge of the knife to scrape down the milk; set aside.

Cook the bacon in a large skillet, remove bacon and set aside to chop, but leave drippings in the skillet. Add sausage or ham to drippings, if using, and cook over medium high until browned. Remove with a slotted spoon and transfer to the beans. Add the okra to the drippings and cook for about 3 minutes or until lightly browned. Add onion and bell pepper and cook another 4 minutes until softened; add the garlic and cook another minute.

Add the corn, sugar, butter beans, meat and seasonings to the skillet. Add some of the reserved cooking water, a little at a time, only if mixture is too dry. Reduce heat to medium low, cook and stir until everything is heated through, add tomatoes, bacon and parsley. Stir in butter or cream until warmed through; taste and adjust seasonings as needed. Serve immediately

Fried Green Tomatoes

Ingredients

- 2 large green tomatoes, or more as needed, preferably right off the vine
- Kosher salt and freshly cracked pepper, *to taste*
- 1 cup or more cooking oil, bacon drippings or a combination
- 1 cup buttermilk, *or enough to cover*
- 1 cup cornmeal
- 3/4 cup all-purpose flour, *divided*
- 1/4 to 1/2 teaspoon Cajun seasoning (Chef Stacks Recipe), *or to taste, optional*

How to make it

Place a rack over a pan covered in paper towels; set aside. Slice the tomatoes into thick slices - 1/4 inch to 1/2 inch thick. Season generously with salt and pepper and let sit for 5 minutes.

Heat bacon fat or oil over medium high heat. Place buttermilk in a small bowl. Mix the corn meal with 1/4 cup of the flour and Cajun seasoning on a plate. Dip tomato slices in the remaining flour, shake off, then pass through buttermilk letting excess drip away before finally dredging in the cornmeal mixture, coating both sides and edges. Place immediately into the hot fat, frying for about 3 to 5 minutes per side, or until golden brown, turning only once. Don't crowd the pan ... give them plenty of room to groove!

Drain on the rack, sprinkle immediately with kosher salt as they come out of the pan and serve right away. Can also place into a low oven to keep warm if necessary.

Continue with remaining slices, adding additional bacon fat to the skillet as needed. Tomatoes should be crisp, not soggy.

Southern Fried Corn

Ingredients

- 4 slices of bacon
- 10-12 ears of white, yellow or bi-color corn on the cob, shucked ,stripped and_scraped
- 1/2 tablespoon of granulated sugar
- 4 tablespoons of unsalted butter
- Up to 1/2 cup of whole milk, half and half, or heavy cream, *optional*
- Fresh cracked black pepper, *to taste*
- Sea salt, *only if needed* (taste first!)
- Fresh herbs, such as parsley, *to garnish*, *optional*

Directions

In a large cast iron skillet, chop bacon and cook to crisp; remove and set aside, reserving the drippings in the skillet. While that is cooking, clean the corn, except remove only the tops of the corn kernels. Then, using the blunt side of the knife, scrape the remaining pulp and milk from the cob. Sprinkle the kernels with the sugar; stir and set aside.

In the same skillet that you fried the bacon in, add all of the butter to the bacon drippings and melt over medium heat. Add all of the corn, pulp and juices, and about 1 tablespoon of the cream. Continue cooking over medium low heat, stirring often and adding additional cream as the corn begins to dry, just enough to keep the corn slightly moist. Reduce to low and cook about 30 minutes, or until corn is tender. Add pepper and half of the bacon; taste and adjust for salt only as needed. Transfer corn to

serving dish, crumble remaining bacon on top and sprinkle with parsley, if desired. Recipe may easily be halved.

CHEF STACK's Notes: **Turn heat up to medium high at the end to brown, if desired. Substitute well-drained canned or frozen corn when fresh is out of season - 3/4 cup of kernels is roughly equal to 1 ear. Allow frozen corn to thaw slightly before using it and for canned or frozen, cook only until corn is heated through well**

MAQUE CHOUX

Ingredients

- 2 tablespoons of unsalted butter
- 1/4 cup of chopped onion
- 1/4 cup of chopped green bell pepper
- 1 (15 ounce) can of whole kernel corn, *drained*
- 1/4 teaspoon of dried basil
- Kosher salt and freshly cracked black pepper, *to taste*
- 1 large tomato, peeled and chopped
- 2 teaspoons of granulated sugar, *optional*

Instructions

Melt butter in a skillet and sauté the onion and bell pepper until softened, about 5 minutes. Add the corn, cover and cook on low for 10 minutes. Stir in the tomato and sugar, cover and continue cooking another 5 minutes.

CHEF STACK's Notes: When fresh corn is in season, substitute about 2 medium to large sized ears. Use the no husk micro wave technic to pre-cook it, or allow time for the raw corn to cook in the skillet. Can substitute 1 (10 ounce) package of frozen corn and/or one (15 ounce) can of diced tomatoes, drained. I didn't peel my tomato, and while I did find a few curls of tomato skin it wasn't too troublesome for us. For variety, sauté 2 slices of bacon, cut up until tender, then sauté the veggies in the bacon drippings. Add butter at the end if desired.

Crawfish Maque Choux: Add one pound of crawfish tails, with any fats, with the corn.

Okra, Corn and Tomatoes Variation: **Sauté 2 cups of frozen okra in with the veggies, add remaining ingredients and proceed.**

Southern Style Creamed peas

Ingredients

- 2 tablespoons of butter
- 4 tablespoons of bacon fat
- 4 tablespoons of all purpose flour
- 1/2 of an onion, finely chopped
- 2 cans of peas, any kind, undrained (petit pois recommended)
- 1 teaspoon of granulated sugar
- 1/4 teaspoon of Cajun seasoning (Chef Stacks Recipe) *or to taste*, *optional*
- 2 pinches of kosher salt
- 1/4 teaspoon of freshly cracked black pepper, *or to taste*

Instructions

In a heavy medium size saucepan, melt the butter and the bacon fat together using a slightly over medium heat setting. Add the flour and stir continually until all of the flour is incorporated. Reduce heat to medium and continue stirring until roux has turned a medium blond color.

Remove the roux from the heat and quickly stir in the chopped onion. Return to the stove and continue cooking, stirring constantly, for about 3 minutes. Add the peas, liquid and all, then the sugar, Cajun seasoning, salt and pepper and bring up to a boil. Reduce heat to low, cover and simmer for 15 minutes.

Big Balla Chicken Mac N Cheese

Ingredients

- 1/2 (16-oz.) package Elbow pasta
- 2 tablespoons butter
- 1 medium onion, diced
- 1 green bell pepper, diced
- 1 (10-oz.) can diced tomatoes and green chilies
- 1 (8-oz.) package pasteurized prepared cheese product, cubed
- 3 cups chopped cooked chicken
- 1 (10 3/4-oz.) can cream of chicken soup
- 1/2 cup sour cream
- 1 teaspoon chili powder
- 1/2 teaspoon ground cumin
- 1 1/2 cups (6 oz.) shredded Cheddar cheese

How to make it

- Preheat oven to 350°. Prepare pasta according to package directions.
- Meanwhile, melt butter in a large Dutch oven over medium-high heat. Add onion and bell pepper, and sauté 5 minutes or until tender. Stir in tomatoes and green chilies and prepared cheese product; cook, stirring constantly, 2 minutes or until cheese melts. Stir in chicken, next 4 ingredients, and hot cooked pasta until blended. Spoon mixture into a lightly greased 10-inch cast-iron skillet or 11- x 7-inch baking dish; sprinkle with shredded Cheddar cheese.
- Bake at 350° for 25 to 30 minutes or until bubbly.

Slap Ya Momma
Sweet Potatoes

Ingredients:

- **2 cups water**
- **2 cups fine granulated sugar**
- **4 tablespoons butter**
- **1 teaspoon lemon juice**
- **1/2 teaspoon ground nutmeg**
- **1/4 teaspoon cinnamon**
- **8 small yams or sweet potatoes**

How to make it

- **Peel outer skin from yams or sweet potatoes and slice into 1/2 to 3/4 inch thick circles. Rinse in cold water, allow to drain then set aside for later use.**
- **In a medium pot, bring water and sugar to a rolling boil, add butter, lemon juice, nutmeg, cinnamon and sliced yams or sweet potatoes. Return to boil, cover pot and reduce heat to simmer.**
- **Cook yams or sweet potatoes for 35 to 45 minutes until tender. Gentle stir throughout cooking.**

Mmm Those Hushpuppies

Ingredients

- 2 1/4 cups self-rising white cornmeal mix
- 1/2 cup chopped green bell pepper
- 1/2 medium onion, chopped
- 1 teaspoon salt
- 1/4 teaspoon ground red pepper
- 1/2 teaspoon ground black pepper
- 1 cup buttermilk
- 2 large eggs
- Vegetable oil

How to make it

- Combine first 6 ingredients in a bowl; make a well in center of mixture.
- Whisk together buttermilk and eggs; add to dry ingredients, stirring just until moistened. Let mixture stand 30 minutes.
- Pour oil to a depth of 2 inches into a Dutch oven; heat to 375°.
- Drop batter by heaping teaspoonful's into hot oil. Fry, in batches, 2 minutes on each side or until golden. Drain on wire racks over paper towels; serve hot.

There's no bread like Cornbread

Ingredients

- 1-1/2 cups yellow corn meal
- 1-1/2 cups general all purpose flour
- 4 tablespoons baking powder
- 2 tablespoons sugar
- 1 teaspoon salt
- 1-1/2 cups milk
- 2 eggs
- 2 tablespoons vegetable oil
- 2 tablespoons melted butter

How To make it

As always the key to great cooking is to be prepared and to use quality ingredients.

- You can start off by greasing your cast iron skillet with a little vegetable oil. Set the oven to 425 degrees and heat your skillet. If you don't have the cast iron skillet go head and use a iron baking pan.
- Blend corn meal, flour, baking powered and sugar in a mixing bowl. In another bowl Whisk together your milk, eggs and

melted butter. Make the cornbread batter by mixing your dry and wet ingredients together thoroughly.

- **Next using oven mittens, carefully remove the cast iron skillet from the oven. Using a kitchen basting brush or whatever you have available coat the inside of your skillet with vegetable oil.**
- **Pour batter into the skillet and return to oven. Bake for about half an hour or until a wooden tooth pick inserted in the center comes out clean. The finished product will be golden brown.**

Homemade Biscuits

Ingredients

- 2 cups all purpose flour, unbleached
- 4 teaspoons baking powder
- 1/2 teaspoon salt
- Pinch of garlic
- 2 tablespoons shortening
- 3/4 cup butter milk

Cookware and Utensils:

- 1 biscuit cutter but in our house momma used a cup
- 1 non stick baking sheet
- 1 cutting or pastry board
- 1 glass or ceramic mixing bowl
- 1 measuring cup
- 1 butter knife

Recipe Instructions:

As always the key to great cooking is to be prepared and to use quality ingredients.

- Preheat oven to 450 degrees.
- Start by mixing and then shifting the dry ingredients. Rub the shortening into the mixture using your fingertips. Next

gradually add milk while stirring mixture with a knife. A soft dough will form.

- **Turn dough onto a floured cutting or pastry board. Work dough to one-half inch thickness and cut using biscuit cutter. Place biscuits on baking sheet, not allowing the dough to touch.**

- **Bake at 450 degrees for 10 to 15 minutes.**

Blackeyed Peas Recipe

Recipe Ingredients:

- 1 bag (1 lbs) dry black eyed peas
- 3 pieces of thick bacon
- 2 tablespoons olive oil
- 1 tablespoon chopped onion
- 1/2 teaspoon garlic powder
- 1/4 teaspoon crushed red pepper
- 1/4 teaspoon black pepper

Cookware and Utensils:

- 1 large pot or dutch oven
- 1 cooking Spoon

Recipe Instructions:

As always the key to great cooking is being prepared and to use quality ingredients.

- You can pick up a bag of dry blackeyed peas at your local grocery store. Start with a small bag of peas, about 1 pound. This should produce about 5-6 cups of cooked beans.
- Sorting and rinsing your peas is very simple. Sort through your peas removing any defective peas, dirt or debris that may

be present. Place the peas in a colander and rinse several times.

- **In order to make that perfect dish you have to soak your peas before cooking. After a good rinsing place peas in pot and cover with at least 3 inches of water. Place peas in your refrigerator and soak peas overnight.**
- **After the peas have soaked overnight discard the water. Rinse peas one finally time. Place peas into a large pot or dutch oven and cover with two inches of fresh water. Bring water to a boil then add other ingredients. Add lid to your pot and simmer 2 hours until peas are tender.**

Chef Stacks Notes -Do not let water cook out. Add additionally seasoning to taste if required.

BBQ Baked beans

Ingredients:

- **2 lbs navy beans**
- **8 slices hickory bacon, cut crosswise into thin strips**
- **2 cups chopped onion**
- **2 large garlic cloves, peeled and minced**
- **1-1/2 cups ketchup**
- **2 cups dark brown sugar, packed**
- **2 teaspoons mustard powder**
- **2 tablespoons red chili powder, ground**

Recipe Instructions:

- **Pick through navy beans to remove any foreign objects. Place beans into large pot, cover with water and soak overnight. When ready to cook pour off water, replace with fresh water. Cook beans over medium-high heat until tender. Remove pot from heat, drain water from beans and sit pot aside.**
- **Preheat oven to 325 degrees Fahrenheit.**
- **While oven is preheating, prepare bacon strips by frying in a skillet over medium heat. Cook and stir bacon about 3 minutes until lightly browned. Add in onion and garlic, continuing to cook and stir until onions are transparent. Pour bacon and**

onion mixture along with any grease that forms into a large mixing bowl.

- **In large mixing bowl, add to bacon and onion mixture the remaining ingredients consisting of ketchup, brown sugar, mustard powder and red chili powder. Now pour in cooked navy beans. Combine and mix all ingredients thoroughly.**
- **Pour baked beans mixture into a large 4 quart baking dish. Bake your homemade baked beans uncovered for 3 hours until done.**

Chapter 3 Desserts

Need I say more, this is where my momma really shined, desserts would have everyone stopping by our house for a plate .

7 up pound cake

Ingredients

- 1 cup unsalted butter, softened
- ½ cup butter-flavored shortening
- 3 cups granulated sugar
- 5 large eggs, room temperature
- 1 teaspoon vanilla extract
- 1 teaspoon lemon extract
- Zest of 1 lemon
- Zest of 1 lime
- 3 cups all-purpose flour, sifted
- ½ teaspoon salt
- ¼ cup heavy whipping cream
- 1 cup 7-Up soda
- 7-up glaze (1 cup of powdered sugar mixed with 2 tablespoons of 7- up)

Instructions

- Preheat oven to 325 F.
- Generously grease and lightly flour a bundt pan. Set aside.
- In a large bowl, cream together butter, shortening and sugar.
- Mix in the eggs one at a time.
- Fold in the vanilla extract and lemon extract.
- Fold in the lemon zest and lime zest.
- Gradually add in the flour and salt and mix until combined.
- Mix in the heavy whipping cream and 7-up until well combined and batter is fluffy.
- Spoon batter into bundt pan.
- Bake for 1 hour and 10-15 minutes (check on it after the 1 hour mark) or until knife inserted into middle comes out clean.
- Let cake sit in pan until pan is warm to the touch.
- Remove from pan and place on a cooling rack until completely cooled.
- Drizzle with 7-up glaze if desired.

Bourbon Bread pudding

Ingredients

- Pudding:
- 2 tablespoons butter, softened
- 4 cups fat-free milk
- 9 cups (1/2-inch) cubed French bread
- 2 cups sugar
- 2 teaspoons vanilla extract
- 4 large egg whites
- 1 large egg
- 1/2 cup raisins
- Sauce:
- 3/4 cup sugar
- 6 tablespoons butter
- 1 large egg
- 1/4 cup bourbon

How to Make It

• Preheat oven to 350°.

• To prepare pudding, spread 2 tablespoons butter onto bottom and sides of a 13 x 9-inch baking dish. Set aside.

•Heat milk in a heavy saucepan over medium-high heat to 180° or until tiny bubbles form around edge (do not boil). Place bread in a large bowl; pour hot milk over bread.

•Combine 2 cups sugar and next 3 ingredients (through 1 egg) in a medium bowl, stirring with a whisk until well blended. Gradually add the egg mixture to milk mixture, stirring constantly with a whisk. Stir in raisins; pour into prepared dish. Place dish in a roasting pan; add hot water to pan to a depth of 1/2 inch. Bake at 350° for 50 minutes or until browned and set.

•To prepare sauce, combine 3/4 cup sugar, 6 tablespoons butter, and 1 egg in a small, heavy saucepan over low heat. Cook 4 minutes or until a candy thermometer registers 165° and mixture is thick, stirring constantly. Remove from heat; stir in bourbon.

Sweet Potato Pie Recipe

Recipe Ingredients:

- **3 frozen unbaked 8 or 9 inch single crust pie shells**
- **4 pounds uncooked and un-peeled sweet potatoes**
- **1/2 cup (1 stick) butter**
- **1/2 cup pure finely granulated sugar**
- **1/2 cup light brown sugar (packed)**
- **3 large eggs**
- **2 cups whole milk**
- **1 tablespoon vanilla extract**
- **1/2 teaspoon salt**
- **1/4 teaspoon nutmeg**

Cookware and Utensils:

- **1 measuring cup**
- **1 mixing bowl**
- **1 cooking blender**
- **1 stirring spoon**

Recipe Instructions:

- **First, hand wash your sweet potatoes. After a complete washing, boil the sweet potatoes until they are tender. Once potatoes are tender drain and allow them to cool before peeling and mashing. Blend your sweet potatoes in mixing bowl with a blender to remove strings.**
- **While you are cooking the sweet potatoes go ahead and place your butter on the kitchen countertop and allow to soften.**

- **After the potatoes are ready, go ahead and preheat your oven to 350.**
- **Next cream the softened butter with both sugars. Mix in the blended sweet potatoes and continue to mix while adding the eggs one at a time. Finally, add your milk, vanilla extract, nutmeg and salt and mix thoroughly.**
- **Finally, pour mixture evenly into your three frozen unbaked pie shells. Bake for 1 hour and 30 minutes at 350 degrees on your center oven rack.**

Preparation Time = approx 1 hour and 40 minutes

Cooking Time = 1 hour and 30 minutes

Soul Food Peach Cobbler Recipe

Recipe Ingredients:

- **3 tbsp butter**
- **1/2 cup self rising flour**
- **1/2 cup pure fine granulated sugar**
- **1/2 cup whole milk**
- **1/2 teaspoon vanilla extract**
- **1-1/2 cup canned sliced peaches w/juice**

Cookware and Utensils:

- **1 - Measuring cup**
- **1 - 8.5x4.5x2.5in Baking pan**
- **1 – Mixing bowl**

1 – Stirring spoon

Recipe Instructions:

- **Preheat oven to 350 degrees Fahrenheit. While you're preheating your oven, go ahead and melt 3 tablespoons of butter into a baking pan.**
- **Combine flour and sugar into a mixing bowl and stir briefly. Next add whole milk and vanilla extract, then mix thoroughly. By now your oven should be preheated and your butter melted.**
- **After the butter has melted, pour your mixture to the baking pan. Next evenly distribute your sliced peaches over the mixture. Do not stir. Bake at 350 degrees, in the center of your oven for 1**

hour until peach cobbler is golden brown. This recipe will feed 4 to 5 people.

Preparation Time = 8 minutes Cooking Time = 1 hour until golden brown

Red Velvet Cake Recipe

Recipe Ingredients:

Cake:

- **2 cups pure fine granulated sugar**
- **2 cups general purpose flour**
- **1 teaspoon baking soda**
- **1/2 teaspoon salt**
- **1 cup vegetable oil**
- **1 cup butter milk**
- **3 eggs**
- **1-1/2 bottle red food coloring (1.5 fluid oz)**
- **1 teaspoon vanilla extract**
- **1 teaspoon white vinegar**

Icing/Frosting:

- **1 box confectioners sugar (16 oz)**
- **1 cup finely chopped pecans**
- **1 stick margarine (8 tbsp or 1/2 cup)**
- **1 large cream cheese (8 oz)**

Cookware and Utensils:

- **2 stainless steel cake pans (8 or 9")**
- **1 measuring cup**
- **1 mixing bowl**
- **1 stirring spoon**
- **1 cooking bender**

Recipe Instructions:

As always the key to great cooking is to be prepared and use quality ingredients.

How to Prepare Cake:

- **Preheat oven to 350 degrees Fahrenheit.**
- **Combine and stir sugar, flour, baking soda and salt into mixing bowl. Next add your wet**

ingredients (vegetable oil, butter milk, eggs, red food coloring, vanilla extract, and white vinegar) one at a time, beating on low to medium speed, continuously beating mixture thoroughly after adding each additional ingredient.

- Spray or grease both pans with a light coat of vegetable oil to stop sticking. Pour completed mixture evenly into your two single layered cake pans. Bake for about 30 minutes at 350 degrees on your center oven rack.
- Cake is done when wooden toothpick inserted into center of cake comes out clean. Let cake cool completely before adding your homemade Icing.

How to Prepare Icing:

While the cake is cooling, here is how to make your Icing.

- Combine confectioners sugar and finely chopped pecans into a mixing bowl and stir with spoon.
- Next add your softened margarine and cream cheese one at a time into the mixing bowl containing the sugar and chopped pecans. Using a cooking blender, mix thoroughly after each ingredient is added.
- Place icing into your refrigerator, since the icing should be applied to cake in a cold state.

Preparation Time = 50 minutes

Cooking Time = about 30 minutes

Red Velvet Cake Recipe

Recipe Ingredients:

Cake:

- 2 cups pure fine granulated sugar
- 2 cups general purpose flour
- 1 teaspoon baking soda
- 1/2 teaspoon salt
- 1 cup vegetable oil
- 1 cup butter milk
- 3 eggs
- 1-1/2 bottle red food coloring (1.5 fluid oz)
- 1 teaspoon vanilla extract
- 1 teaspoon white vinegar

Icing/Frosting:

- 1 box confectioners sugar (16 oz)
- 1 cup finely chopped pecans
- 1 stick margarine (8 tbsp or 1/2 cup)
- 1 large cream cheese (8 oz)

Cookware and Utensils:

- 2 stainless steel cake pans (8 or 9")
- 1 measuring cup
- 1 mixing bowl
- 1 stirring spoon
- 1 cooking bender

Recipe Instructions:

As always the key to great cooking is to be prepared and use quality ingredients.

How to Prepare Cake:

- Preheat oven to 350 degrees Fahrenheit.
- Combine and stir sugar, flour, baking soda

and salt into mixing bowl. Next add your wet ingredients (vegetable oil, butter milk, eggs, red food coloring, vanilla extract, and white vinegar) one at a time, beating on low to medium speed, continuously beating mixture thoroughly after adding each additional ingredient.

- Spray or grease both pans with a light coat of vegetable oil to stop sticking. Pour completed mixture evenly into your two single layered cake pans. Bake for about 30 minutes at 350 degrees on your center oven rack.
- Cake is done when wooden toothpick inserted into center of cake comes out clean. Let cake cool completely before adding your homemade Icing.

How to Prepare Icing:

While the cake is cooling, here is how to make your Icing.

- Combine confectioners sugar and finely chopped pecans into a mixing bowl and stir with spoon.
- Next add your softened margarine and cream cheese one at a time into the mixing bowl containing the sugar and chopped pecans. Using a cooking blender, mix thoroughly after each ingredient is added.
- Place icing into your refrigerator, since the icing should be applied to cake in a cold state.

Preparation Time = 50 minutes

Cooking Time = about 30 minutes

Banana Pudding Recipe

Recipe Ingredients:

- **2 large boxes of cook and serve vanilla pudding**
- **6 cups whole milk**
- **1 box of vanilla wafers**
- **6-8 fresh bananas**

Cookware and Utensils:

- **1 measuring cup**
- **1 medium boiling pot**
- **1 serving bowl**
- **1 stirring spoon**

Recipe Instructions:

- **As always the key to great cooking is preparation and quality ingredients.**
- **First, mix pudding and milk together. Second, bring mixture to boil over medium-high heat, stirring constantly until pudding thickens. Remove pudding from heat and allow to cool briefly. While your pudding is cooling go ahead and cut your bananas into quarter-inch thick slices. Once the bananas are sliced it's time to layer the pudding.**
- **Using a serving bowl of your choice, start**

with a layer of wafers on the bottom. Next add bananas then pudding. Repeat the process ending with a layer of vanilla wafers on top. Be sure to save your best looking wafers for the top layer.

- **Refrigerate and serve cold unless you like your pudding hot. This dessert is also great topped with whipped cream.**

Preparation Time = 10 minutes
Cooking Time = 20 minutes

Lemon Meringue Pie

Recipe Ingredients:

- **1 x 9-inch frozen pie shell**

Lemon Filling:

- **1-1/4 cups granulated sugar**
- **6 tablespoons cornstarch**
- **1/8 teaspoon salt**
- **grated rind of 1 lemon**
- **2 cups boiling water**
- **4 tablespoons butter**
- **3 egg yolks**
- **1/2 cup fresh lemon juice**

Meringue:

- **3 egg whites**
- **pinch of salt**
- **1 teaspoon lemon juice**
- **6 tablespoons granulated sugar**

Recipe Instructions:

- **Bake pie shell according to package directions until pie crust is lightly brown. Remove baked pie shell from oven and cool on a rack. Raise oven temperature to 400 degree Fahrenheit.**

- **First let's prepare the <u>lemon filling</u>. Combine sugar, cornstarch, salt, grated lemon rind and water in heavy bottom saucepan. Cook, stirring constantly over medium heat until mixture comes to a boil. Once mixture begins to boil continue to stir for another minute. Remove from heat and add butter to sugar mixture, but do not stir.**
- **Separate egg whites from yolks and place in different bowls.**
- **Add lemon juice to egg yolks and whisk together using a wire whisk or fork. Pour this mixture into hot sugar mixture and blend thoroughly. Lemon filling is complete.**
- **Pour lemon filling into lightly browned pie shell and bake at 400°F for 10 minutes.**
- **As soon as you place pie in oven it's time to prepare the meringue. Add salt to bowl containing egg whites and beat until soft peaks form. Next add lemon juice, then gradually mix in sugar until meringue is stiff.**
- **Remove pie from oven and spoon meringue over the lemon pie filling after it has baked for 10 minutes. For best results form a mound with the meringue in the center of the pie, then spread out evenly to the outer edges.**

- **Set oven temperature to 350 degree Fahrenheit. Place pie back into oven and continue baking until meringue is lightly browned.**

Chapter 4

Beverages

And yes we had refreshing drinks for the young and the adults , I couldn’t wait till I was old enough for the adult drinks.

MOMMAS SOUTHERN SWEET TEA

Ingredients

- 2 quarts of water
- 1/2 to 3/4 cup of granulated sugar, *or to taste*
- 5 or 6 individual Luzianne tea bags

Instructions

Combine water and sugar in a large saucepan, whisk together and bring to a boil. Remove from heat, add the tea bags, cover and steep for 15 minutes. Remove tea bags, let cool slightly, then pour into a half gallon pitcher. Do not add additional water or ice. Pour over ice filled glasses to serve.

CHEF STACK'S Notes: Double for a gallon. You can also prepare the simple syrup in the microwave if you have a large enough lidded microwave safe container. Six teabags makes a more robust flavor; two family sized tea bags may be substituted.

Cane Sugar Sweet Iced Tea: Substitute turbinado 100% pure, raw cane sugar (like Sugar in the Raw brand) for the granulated sugar. It's my favorite sugar to use.

Sweet Tea Syrup Concentrate: Prepare simple syrup as above except use 3 cups each of water and sugar and increase tea bags to 10-12, depending on strength desired. Steep 15 minutes and let cool. Do not add ice or water. Refrigerate. Use 3/4 cup of the syrup (or to taste) to 6 cups of water to a make 1-1/2 quart pitcher. For individual glasses, fill with ice and top off

with ice cold water, spooning in several tablespoons according to color and taste.

MOMMAS HOT DAY LEMONAIDE

Ingredients

- 1/2 cup of boiling water
- 1-1/2 cups of granulated sugar
- 1-1/2 cups of freshly squeezed lemon juice (about 8 lemons)
- Zest of one lemon
- 5 cups of cold water
- Additional sliced lemon for garnish, *optional*

Instructions

Make a simple syrup by bringing 1/2 cup of water and the sugar to a boil. Boil for 3 minutes, stirring regularly and heating until mixture becomes clear and slightly thickened. Set mixture aside to cool.

Using a microplane, zest one of the lemons; set aside. Squeeze the juice from about 8 lemons or until you have 1-1/2 cups of lemon juice. Add the juice to a 2 quart pitcher along with the zest and cold water. Whisk in the cooled simple syrup and refrigerate overnight or for at least 8 hours. Serve in tall glasses over ice and garnish with lemon slices, if desired.

Lemon-Lime: Add in 1/2 cup of fresh lime juice and lime slices.

Pink Lemonade: Add 1/8 to 1/4 cup grenadine, cranberry or pomegranate juice, or to taste.

Strawberry Lemonade: Prepare as above, except process 1 pound of rinsed and hulled strawberries in a blender or food processor. Strain, using a sieve, into the prepared lemonade.

Blueberry Lemonade: **Prepare simple syrup as above. Add in 1 cup of fresh blueberries, reduce to a simmer and cook until berries pop and release. Strain, using a sieve and set aside to cool. Whisk into the lemonade as above.**

Blackberry Lemonade: **Prepare simple syrup as above. Process 2 cups of blackberries in a blender or food processor and strain, using a sieve, into the prepared lemonade.**

Peach Lemonade: **Prepare simple syrup as above. Process 1-1/2 pounds of fresh peaches, peeled, pitted and sliced in a blender or food processor. Strain, using a sieve, into the prepared lemonade.**

Birthday party punch

Ingredients

- 6 (3 ounce) packages of Jello gelatin (strawberry, lemon, lime, raspberry, etc.)
- 6 cups of boiling water
- 4 cups of granulated sugar
- 6 cups of cold water
- 3 large cans of frozen orange juice
- 3 large cans of frozen lemonade
- 3 large cans of pineapple juice
- 3 large bottles of ginger ale, or liters of 7-up or Sprite or any combination of them
- 4 quarts of pineapple or other sherbet, optional
- Fresh fruit, flash frozen individually, optional (see note in recipe)

Instructions

In a very large pot or other container, dissolve the Jello in the boiling water; add the sugar, stirring until dissolved, then add the cold water. Mix the orange juice according to the package directions and pour into the Jello mixture; stir. Repeat with the lemonade. DO NOT add the ginger ale or 7-up/Sprite at this stage!! That will be added just before serving. Stir to blend well and transfer into individual storage containers to chill. Well washed, leftover milk jugs or orange juice cartons work well for this. Chill for at least 24 hours.

GROWN FOLKS ICE TEA

Ingredients

- 1 quart size Mason jar, or 2 pints
- 1 ounce of light rum
- 1 ounce of vodka
- 1 ounce of gin
- 4 ounces of freshly squeezed lemon juice or lemonade
- 3 ounces of unsweetened iced tea recipe
- 1 to 2 ounces of simple syrup, to taste
- Sprigs of mint, for garnish
- Slices of lemon, for garnish

Instructions

Fill a quart Mason jar with ice. Add the rum, vodka and gin, lemon juice or lemonade, iced tea and simple syrup. Stir thoroughly, taste and adjust sweetness if needed; garnish with a slice of lemon and sprig of mint. As always, drink responsibly and don't drink and drive.

Makes one, unless you feel like sharin'.

CHEF STACK'S NOTE: **I made** one recipe of iced tea**, except I did not pour it over ice into a pitcher. Simply remove the tea bags and use the unsweetened concentrate in the cocktail.**

Tipsy Palmer: **Omit rum, vodka and gin, substituting bourbon, Maker's Mark recommended.**

DERBY DAYS MINT JULIP

Ingredients

- 1 dozen fresh mint leaves, plus a few sprigs for garnish
- 2 tablespoons of simple syrup
- 2 ounces of Bourbon
- 1 ounce of Dark Rum
- Crushed ice

Instructions

Chill a traditional silver julep glass, old fashioned, Collins, or highball glass by placing into the freezer, or jiggling some ice in the glass. Remove ice and lightly muddle the mint and simple syrup together in the bottom of the glass. Top with some of the ice. Stick a straw all the way through the ice to the bottom of the glass where the mint is, then cut the straw off short, just above the top of the glass. Top the ice with the bourbon, then the rum, the remaining ice, and holding the glass along the bottom or top edge, stir vigorously, until the outside of the glass is heavily frosted. Garnish with a sprig of mint right next to the straw so that you get a nice whiff of mint with each sip.

By the Pitcher: **Muddle about 1 cup of mint leaves together with 3/4 cup of simple syrup, more or less to taste, in the bottom of a pitcher. Add 1-1/2 cups of bourbon and 3/4 cup of rum. Add straw to chilled cups and fill with crushed ice, pouring mixture over the top. Makes about 6 depending on size of glasses. Garnish with mint as above.**

I would love to say thank you.

First of all I would like to thank the lord for blessing me with the ability to be able to prepare the amazing dishes that I have learned to make from my family, and pointing me in the right direction with my culinary career.

Next I would like to thank my wife Stacey for being behind me every step of the way.

Next I would like to thank My momma Alice Page for showing me all her secrets , I may have acted like I wasn't listening but I was momma I love you.

Next I would like to thank all my kids your all my hearts and you are the reason that I strive for perfection, my brother Dorsey and Roberto A-K-A YellowSky for always having my back and making my graphics love you guys

Next to all of my nieces and nephews, I have always wanted to be a good role model and I hope I did a good job. And Lastly to All my fans, followers and supporters without all of you I would be nothing . Thank you and I love you all.

Chef Stackz

Made in the USA
San Bernardino, CA
01 November 2018